The
World War I
Armistice

11 November 1918

The World War I Armistice

John Malam

CHERRYTREE
BOOKS

A Cherrytree Book

First published 2003
by CherrytreeBooks
Evans Brothers Limited
2a Portman Mansions
Chiltern Street
London WIU 6NR

First published in 2003

British Library Cataloguing in Publication Data

Malam, John
   WWI - Armistice Day, - (Dates with history)
   I. Armistice Day - Juvenile literature 2. World War,
   1914-1918 - Juvenile literature
   I. Title
   940.4'39

ISBN 1842342002

To contact the author, send an email to:
johnmalam@aol.com

Series Editor: Louise John
Editor: Mary-Jane Wilkins
Designer: Mark Holt
Maps: Tim Smith

Picture credits:
Corbis: 11, 21
John Malam: 24, 25, 26, 28, 36, 37, 41.
Mary Evans Picture Library: front cover, 12, 13, 14, 16,
    17, 19, 23, 29, 31, 32, 33, 34.
Popperfoto: 15, 20, 22, 30, 35, 39
Topham Picturepoint: 27

Contents

Where war ended

The Forest of Compiègne is in north-east France, about 80 km north of Paris. It is a beautiful woodland area, visited each year by walkers, campers, cyclists and horse-riders. As today's tourists enjoy the forest and splendid views of the surrounding countryside, some stumble across a clearing amid the oak and beech trees. Others come here already knowing about this open space, and they seek it out.

The forest clearing is a wide, circular area. It marks a place where history was made – the very place where, in 1918, the Great War officially ended. Nowadays we refer to this terrible conflict as World War 1.

The peaceful Forest of Compiègne today. This is the forest where World War 1 ended in 1918.

The day the armistice was signed

At five o'clock on the morning of 11 November 1918, a group of high-ranking German politicians and military officers entered a railway carriage in the Forest of Compiègne. They were met by delegates from the countries with which they had been at war. Three days earlier the French, British and Americans had prepared

Military leaders whose armies defeated Germany, outside the carriage where the armistice was signed.

Officials from Germany about to sign the armistice document.

an **armistice** document which they demanded the
Germans accept within three days. Inside the carriage
the Germans signed the surrender document put before
them. The document signalled that the war would stop in
six hours' time, at the eleventh hour of the eleventh day
of the eleventh month of 1918.

World War I, fought between 1914 and 1918, was the
first truly international war. Although much of the fighting
took place on the fields of northern France and Belgium,
many nations from around the world had been drawn
into it. It was a modern war, a war fought with new
weapons, a war that claimed the lives of millions of
people, a war that changed the map of western Europe.
It was, so people said, the war to end all wars.

Blood on the streets

An event on the streets of Sarajevo, the capital of Bosnia, south-east Europe, led to the start of World War I. On 28 June 1914, Sarajevo had important visitors – the **heir** to the throne of the Austro-Hungarian empire, Archduke Franz Ferdinand, and his wife, Sophie. But not everyone in the city welcomed them.

Bosnia had been part of the Austro-Hungarian empire since 1878. It was a vast empire that belonged to Austria-Hungary, and it covered much of central Europe. However, there were many Bosnians who did not want their country to belong to another nation, and they looked for a way of gaining independence.

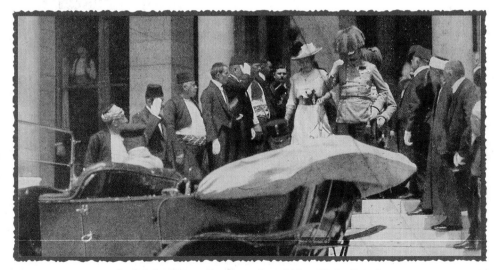

Archduke Franz Ferdinand and his wife in Sarajevo,
on the day of their assassination.

Some Bosnians organised themselves into terrorist groups, with the aim of winning freedom for Bosnia. One group was the Black Hand, and among its members was a young student, 19-year-old Gavrilo Princep.

The day that Archduke Franz Ferdinand visited Sarajevo was seen by **militant** Bosnians as their big chance to send a clear message to Austria-Hungary. They hoped to show how much they wanted freedom for Bosnia by assassinating the Archduke.

A portrait of Gavrilo Princep, a member of the Black Hand terrorist group.

As the open-topped car carrying the visitors drove through the streets of Sarajevo on that fateful June morning, Nedjelko Cabrinovic, a Black Hand terrorist, threw a bomb. It struck Franz Ferdinand on the arm, bounced off the car and exploded in the street, injuring a number of spectators. Cabrinovic was quickly arrested. The car continued on its journey to Sarajevo town hall, where the Archduke had a meeting with the city's mayor as planned.

The assassination

The terrorists' plot seemed to have failed, but an unexpected second chance came their way. After his meeting with the mayor, the Archduke and his wife were driven towards the city museum, but on the way the driver took a wrong turn, and the car had to stop.

It could not have stopped in a worse place, for nearby was Gavrilo Princep. The terrorist, seizing his opportunity, took a pistol from his coat, stepped up to the car, and fired three shots at its passengers. Archduke Franz Ferdinand and Sophie were killed.

Within seconds of firing the fatal shots Princep was caught. He had been instructed to take his own life rather than be arrested, but there was no time for him to turn the gun on himself, or swallow the poison he was carrying.

Princep rushes forward and fires the fatal shots.

Within moments of firing his pistol, Princep (second from right) was arrested.

At his trial Princep was sentenced to serve 20 years in prison. He died in prison in 1918, having served just four years of his sentence.

The assassination came at a time of growing tension in the countries of Europe, and it sent a shockwave through them. There was intense rivalry and mistrust between them, and it was almost inevitable that at some point they would start to fight each other. It was more a question of when fighting would begin, not if it would. Within six weeks of the Archduke's murder, the nations of Europe were at war with each other.

The state of the nations

In 1914, Europe was made up of a few powerful nations, chief of which were Austria-Hungary, France, Germany, Russia and Great Britain. They were wealthy, had strong economies and each wanted to be Europe's leading nation.

No single country was powerful enough to dominate Europe on its own. To support each other, some countries promised help to their neighbours, forming bonds known

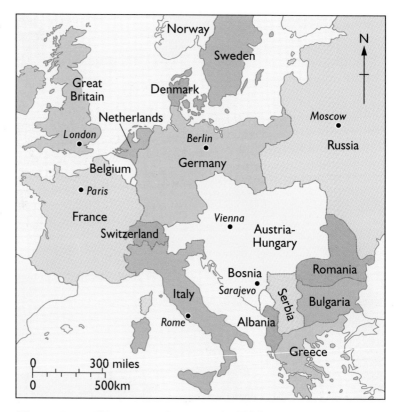

The nations of Europe as they were in 1914.

as **alliances**. The most powerful alliance was between Germany and Austria-Hungary, who became allies in 1879. Their friendship upset both France and Russia, each of whom feared that Germany wanted to invade them.

The alliance between Germany and Austria-Hungary grew stronger in 1882, when they were joined by Italy. Twelve years later, in 1894, France and Russia promised to support each other if either was attacked. In 1906, Britain pledged to defend Belgium, and also France, if either was attacked by Germany.

As nations agreed to help nations, the allied countries emerged as the real powers in Europe. Both Austria-Hungary and Russia wanted to control the Balkan countries (Bosnia and Serbia), while France wanted to win back land lost in 1870 to Prussia, as Germany was then called.

A German battleship being built during the early 1900s.

By the summer of 1914, the peace of Europe was already very fragile – little was needed to disturb it. So the bullets fired by Gavrilo Princep did more than kill a member of a European royal family. They pushed nations into war.

19

Reaction to events in Sarajevo

Austria-Hungary reacted swiftly to the murders of its country's future emperor and empress. It wanted revenge for the double killing, and accused Serbia of being behind the attack in Sarajevo. It was true that the Black Hand terror group had its headquarters in Serbia, and its leader, who had sent Princep and the others to kill Archduke Franz Ferdinand, was a high-ranking officer in the Serbian army.

Serbia, like Bosnia, was a country in the Balkans, and in 1912 it had gained independence from Turkey. Serbia wanted its neighbour Bosnia to break free

Vienna, the prosperous capital city of Austria-Hungary.

from Austro-Hungarian rule. Austria-Hungary
blamed Serbia for stirring up trouble in Bosnia.

To tighten its control over
the Balkan nations, Austria-
Hungary wanted to add
Serbia to its empire. The
murder of Archduke Franz
Ferdinand gave Austria-
Hungary an opportunity to
attack Serbia. The risk was
that an act of aggression
might provoke one of
Serbia's allies to come to
its aid. Austria-Hungary
clearly thought this risk
was worth taking.

The Balkans, in south-east Europe, is a mountainous region.

On 23 July 1914, the government of Austria-Hungary
issued an **ultimatum** to Serbia. It was a strongly-worded
document which called on Serbia to accept responsibility
for the murder of Archduke Franz Ferdinand. Also, Serbia
had to give up its independence and become part of the
Austro-Hungarian empire. This was unacceptable to
Serbia, and the ultimatum was rejected.

On 28 July 1914, Austria-Hungary declared war on Serbia.
From then on there was no going back, and what began
as a minor quarrel between neighbours grew into a war.

The crisis deepens and war begins

The declaration of war by Austria-Hungary tested the strength of the alliances between the nations of Europe. Serbia's **ally** was Russia. When Austria-Hungary declared war on Serbia, Russia immediately promised to help the Serbs. The Russian army was put on stand-by, ready for action. This act of Russian **mobilisation** had a dramatic effect on Germany. The Germans viewed the mobilisation of Russian forces as an act of war against Austria-Hungary, whom Germany supported.

The problem for Germany was this: if it retaliated by putting its own armed forces on stand-by, that would upset France, who would think that Germany was planning to invade it.

Russian troops marching to the railway station in Petrograd (now St Petersburg) in 1914.

With events moving quickly, Germany decided to take the initiative. On 1 August 1914, Germany declared war on Russia, putting the alliance between France and Russia to the test. France had little choice but to stand by its Russian ally, and on 3 August France declared war on both Germany and Austria-Hungary. The same day, German troops invaded Belgium, a neutral country (Belgium did not want to be involved in the war).

When Germany invaded Belgium and threatened France, Britain entered the war on 4 August, keeping a promise to help these countries. Britain, as head of a worldwide empire, brought its overseas colonies into the conflict. Troops from Australia, Canada, India, New Zealand and South Africa prepared to fight for Britain. On the day Britain declared war on Germany, the United States of America announced that it would remain neutral – it would not take sides and would not be drawn into the war.

Most people thought that the war would be over by Christmas. They were very wrong.

Belgian troops put up fierce resistance to the German invasion.

The war in 1914

The German invasion plan was quite simple. The idea was to cross quickly through Belgium and invade France from the north-east. By doing this the Germans would avoid coming into contact with French defences along the border with Germany. Having entered France by the 'back door', the Germans hoped to capture Paris and force the French to surrender. In the event, the Germans' plans didn't work out.

Soldiers of the French army in a trench on the Western Front (see page 25).

The German army did sweep through Belgium, but the further they advanced the harder it became to keep their troops supplied with food and ammunition. The German advance slowed down. On 23 August, at Mons, a town in Belgium, the Germans came under intense fire from British troops and were forced to halt their advance.

24

This was only a temporary setback, and soon the German army reached France, where it met the armies of France and Britain.

Where the sides met, a battle line developed which became known as the **Western Front**. It stretched for around 965 km from the English Channel in the north to Switzerland in the south. Both sides built a series of fortifications along the front, mainly consisting of a network of trenches dug into the ground. Soldiers shot at each other from the trenches, or climbed out of them to go '**over the top**', charging across the open ground between the two sides (known as '**no man's land**') towards the enemy.

The war along the Western Front was fought in this way for the next four years.

A German barbed wire field built between the trenches in no man's land.

Hardly any ground was gained by either side, and millions of men died in conditions of unimaginable horror. Nothing like it had ever been seen before.

The war in 1915

At the beginning of 1915, the war along the Western Front was at a **stalemate**, with neither side able to gain the advantage over the other. This suited Germany, since it allowed its troops to wage war on the **Eastern Front**, where they advanced deep into Russia.

However, the Western Front was not quiet for long, and in the spring France began a huge **offensive** against the German battle lines. The offensive began in February, when French heavy guns fired more than

A heavy gun, called a mortar, belonging to the French army.
Behind are the huge shells it is firing at the German lines.

two million **shell**s at the German lines. This was a non-stop **barrage**, lasting 24 hours a day for six days.

Within a month, 150,000 French soldiers and more than 75,000 German soldiers had been killed. As the offensive spread along the front, the number of casualties increased – 13,000 British soldiers were killed in just three days during March.

The Western Front had become a killing ground. Huge numbers of men were slaughtered, and the armies fought over the same piece of ground time and time again.

In Britain, millions of young men volunteered to join the army, and after a short period of training they were sent to the front. Many soldiers only returned to Britain alive if they got a '**Blighty** one'. This was a soldier's way of saying that he'd been wounded and would be sent home to recover.

A famous poster used in Britain, asking men to volunteer for the army.

27

The terror of poison gas

During a war new types of weapon are often used. In World War I both sides used secret weapons to try to gain an advantage over the other. In 1915, poison gas was used for the first time by the Germans during the Second Battle of Ypres.

On the evening of 22 April 1915, a thick cloud of greenish-yellow gas billowed towards lines of Algerian troops, who were fighting for the French. The gas was released by the Germans from 5,700 cylinders, which were placed a short distance in front of their own lines.

Poison gas released by the German army billows over a battlefield.

It was **chlorine** gas and the wind blew it towards the Algerian soldiers, and away from the Germans.

The chlorine gas was heavier than air, so it sank to the ground and rolled over the troops, who were helpless in their trenches. Some men broke cover, running from the trenches, and were shot dead by the German gunners. Those who stayed behind were soon poisoned by the gas. It made the men's eyes water and blinded them, burned their lungs and made them choke. With no clean air to breathe, many men suffocated.

This gas attack announced the arrival of chemical warfare. Within three days, British troops had been issued with white **gauze** pads fitted with elastic bands. When attacked by

Gas masks offered some protection from the danger of poison gas.

gas, each man had to put a pad over his mouth and nose, in the hope that it would filter out the poison. Later in the war, troops were issued with gas masks that fitted over their heads.

The war in 1916

Some of the heaviest fighting on the Western Front took place in 1916. In February, the German **artillery** bombarded the French forces who were defending the town of Verdun. The Battle of Verdun raged through the year, and became the longest battle of the war.

Big guns like these fired shells over the heads of the French troops and on to the enemy.

The Germans had stronger artillery, and they almost defeated the French. They captured several French forts, and started to advance towards Verdun. However, the French sent a steady stream of new soldiers, and by December they had won back much of the ground lost earlier. Both sides lost many soldiers. The year's rainy weather and the constant explosions of shells had churned the battlefield into a sea of mud. In the mud lay the bodies of one-and-half-million men – an equal number from both sides.

The year's second major battle was the Battle of the Somme, in which British and French forces attacked the Germans. The attack took place along a 29 km front. It began in late June, when 1,000 heavy guns fired non-stop for a week. Then, at 7.30 am on 1 July, 120,000 British troops were given the order to cross no man's land towards the German lines.

Many of the volunteer soldiers had only recently arrived from Britain, and they had little experience of fighting. After the artillery **bombardment**, they did not expect much opposition from the Germans. They were wrong. The Germans were very much alive, and by the end of the day 20,000 British soldiers had been killed. By the time the battle ended in November, the British had moved forward only 10 km.

An artist's view of French troops crossing no man's land during the Battle of the Somme.

Tanks – a new weapon

At dawn on 15 September 1916, during the Battle of the Somme, the British tried out a new weapon. Twenty-four '**landships**' rumbled slowly past the British lines, and the soldiers watched in amazement as they crossed no man's land towards the ranks of Germans.

These armour-plated machines, shaped like lozenges and with caterpillar tracks, earned the nickname '**tanks**'. This was because they had arrived in France disguised as water tanks, to prevent enemy spies discovering their true purpose. British engineers had come up with the

The caterpillar tracks of tanks helped them cross difficult ground.

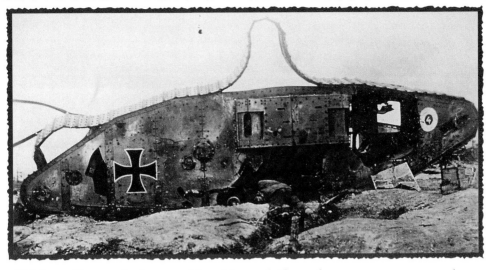

*This huge German tank was captured towards the end
of the war.*

idea for a fighting vehicle that could cross rough ground
after watching the tractors used on American farms.

The first tanks were little more than support vehicles
for the **infantry**. As they moved across the battlefield
they ploughed through **barbed wire** and drove over
enemy trenches, opening up a route for soldiers to move
along. Early tanks had small guns, which were not very
powerful. The tanks were heavy and difficult to
manoeuvre, got stuck in the mud, and often broke down.

The tank attack on the Somme was not very effective,
but it showed how, with improvements, tanks could
become a formidable weapon of war. Within a year,
tanks with thicker armour and bigger guns had become
a common sight on the Western Front.

The war in 1917

A turning point in the war came early in 1917, when German submarines in the Atlantic threatened to attack ships belonging to the United States of America. Until then, America had remained a neutral country, but the Germans believed she was shipping **armaments** to the British, which therefore made her an enemy of Germany. On 6 April, America declared war on Germany, and on 16 June the first American troops and weapons arrived in France.

The year's major battle was the Third Battle of Ypres, though it soon became known simply as Passchendaele, after the village in Belgium which suffered the worst fighting. The battle began on 31 July. It was an attempt by British forces to break through the German lines around Ypres (British troops pronounced it as 'e-pers' or 'y-pers').

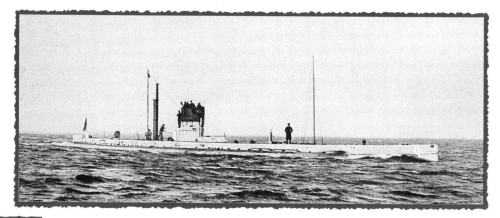

A German submarine surfaces in the Atlantic.

A British stretcher party sink to their knees in mud as they carry a wounded man from the battlefield.

The attack began with the usual bombardment of artillery shells – more than four million of them – followed by an infantry advance. However, the ground was so churned up from the shelling and the relentless rain that the whole area had turned into a sticky sea of mud.

Passchendaele, the village which gave its name to the battle, was literally blown to bits. Barely a trace remained. The battle ended in November, and the sides counted their dead: 250,000 British and 200,000 German soldiers.

The only glimmer of hope in yet another terrible year was that as America had joined in the fighting, the war might soon be over.

The war in 1918

The arrival of American troops in France – 250,000 by early July 1918 – did not bring the war to a rapid end, as many had hoped. The Americans had no experience of war, and at first they lost many men in battle. However, their presence boosted the morale of the war-weary British and French, and demoralised the Germans.

A captured German soldier is searched by American troops.

For a short time in 1918 the Germans pushed the front line more than 50 km further into north-east France, towards the Forest of Compiègne. This was as far as they went, for in July the Second Battle of the Marne began, and the armies of France, Britain and America, supported by tanks, slowly but surely started to push the Germans back. This breakthrough signalled the beginning of the end of the war.

It wasn't only German resistance that crumbled in 1918. One by one Germany's allies were defeated: Bulgaria accepted peace in September, Turkey in October, and

Austria-Hungary in early November. In each case the defeated nation signed an armistice document in which they agreed to lay down their arms, stop fighting and begin peace talks. As Germany's allies surrendered, the German army lost the will to fight. In Germany itself, there were riots in the cities, brought on by a shortage of food. Germany was as good as defeated.

On 8 November a delegation of German officials arrived in the Forest of Compiègne, hoping to negotiate the terms of their surrender. The French, British and Americans had other ideas. They presented the Germans with an armistice document which they said had to be accepted within three days. The German government agreed to it, and so, on 11 November 1918, the armistice was signed, and the war to end all wars was over.

Captured German soldiers heading towards a prison camp.

The aftermath of the war

Many **treaties** were signed after the war had ended and once they had all been agreed the map of Europe had been redrawn. In 1919 Germany was forced to sign the Treaty of Versailles. This said that the German army could have no more than 100,000 troops, that Germany had to pay money to France and Belgium for the damage it had caused, and that Germany's borders were to be changed. Land taken from France in 1870

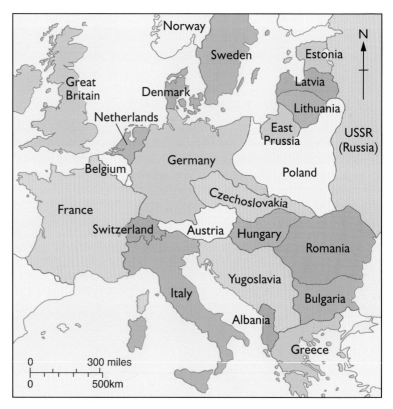

A map of central Europe after World War I.

was to be given back, and Belgium and Denmark were given land near to them. Germans thought the treaty was harsh and unfair. Britain and France, on the other hand, thought that the Germans had got off lightly.

Austria-Hungary signed another treaty – the Treaty of Saint-Germain. This split its former empire to create the countries of Austria and Hungary, and the new countries of Czechoslovakia and Yugoslavia.

Europe after the war was in a state of chaos. Cities lay in ruins and more than ten million people were refugees. A generation of young men had died during the war, and there was a labour shortage.

Thousands of war memorials were built across Europe, in villages and cities, and on the battlefields themselves. These recorded the names of those who gave their lives for their countries. Many fallen

A World War I cemetery at Sanctuary Wood in Belgium.

soldiers were buried in cemeteries close to the battlefields that claimed their young lives. Some, whose bodies were never found, are remembered at their country's Grave of the Unknown Soldier, in London, Paris, Brussels, and in Arlington, USA. On Armistice Day every year, people all over the world remember them.

Timeline

1914   *28 June:* Archduke Franz Ferdinand assassinated in Sarajevo.

1914   *28 July:* Austria-Hungary declares war on Serbia.

1914   *1 August:* Germany declares war on Russia.

1914   *3 August:* Germany declares war on France.

1914   *4 August:* Germany invades Belgium; Britain declares war on Germany and Austria-Hungary.

1914   *23 August:* The German advance is halted at Mons, Belgium, by the British army.

1914   *6–10 September:* The German advance is halted in the First Battle of the Marne, France, by the French army.

1914   *September–November:* The Western Front is established in northern France and Belgium. The sides take up positions in trenches.

1914   *20 October–11 November:* First Battle of Ypres, Belgium

1914   *25 December:* Unofficial Christmas Day truce on the Western Front.

1915   *22 April–24 May:* Second Battle of Ypres, Belgium. First use of chemical weapons in war, by Germany.

1915   *25–28 April:* British troops land at Gallipoli, Turkey.

1915   *7 May:* The passenger liner *Lusitania* is sunk by a German submarine.

1915	*November–December:* After heavy losses, British troops withdraw from Gallipoli, Turkey.
1916	*31 May:* Battle of Jutland, North Sea, the war's only major sea battle.
1916	*1 July–19 November:* Battle of the Somme; first use of tanks, by Britain.
1917	*6 April:* USA declares war on Germany.
1917	*31 July–10 November:* Third Battle of Ypres, Belgium (Passchendaele).
1917	*2–30 September:* German air-raids on London and south-east England.
1918	*15 July–4 August:* Second Battle of the Marne, France. Germans forced to retreat.
1918	*August–September:* Many battles fought along the Western Front. Germans in retreat.
1918	*11 November:* Armistice signed at 5 am; fighting ends at 11 am. The war is over.

The fields of France and Belgium became graveyards for the war's dead.

Glossary

alliance A group of countries or people who come together to support each other.

ally A country or person who has agreed to support another.

armaments Weapons and equipment used by an army.

armistice An agreement during a war to stop fighting.

artillery Large guns used in fighting on land.

barbed wire Wire with spikes, used to make fences and barriers.

barrage Heavy and continuous gunfire.

Blighty Soldiers' slang name for Britain, meaning home.

bombardment An attack which uses many weapons.

chlorine A poisonous green-coloured gas.

Eastern Front The name of the battle line in eastern Europe.

gauze A thin, woven fabric, usually made from cotton.

heir A person who inherits something, such as property or a title, from another person.

infantry Soldiers who fight on foot.

landship The original name given to a tank.

militant A person who uses strong action in support of a cause.

mobilisation Making troops ready to fight in a war.

no man's land The land that lay between the two sides.

offensive A battle begun by one side in a war against the other.

over the top Soldiers went over the top when they left the safety of a trench by hoisting themselves up and climbing out of it.

shell A metal case filled with explosive, which was fired from a large gun.

stalemate A situation in which neither side has an advantage; a draw.

tank An armour-plated heavy machine with caterpillar tracks and one or more guns.

treaty An agreement to do something, made between countries or people.

ultimatum A demand that something must be done.

Western Front The name of the battle line in western Europe.

CASUALTIES OF WORLD WAR I			
Country	*Dead*	*Wounded*	*Missing*	*Total*
Australia	58,150	152,170	–	210,320
Austria-Hungary	922,000	3,600,000	855,283	5,377,283
Belgium	102,000	450,000	–	552,000
Britain	658,700	2,032,150	359,150	3,050,000
Bulgaria	87,500	152,390	27,029	266,919
Canada	56,500	149,700	–	206,200
France	1,359,000	4,200,000	361,650	5,920,650
Germany	1,600,000	4,065,000	103,000	5,768,000
Greece	5,000	21,000	1,000	27,000
India	43,200	65,175	5,875	114,250
Italy	689,000	959,100	–	1,424,660
Japan	300	907	3	1,210
Montenegro	3,000	10,000	7,000	20,000
New Zealand	16,130	40,750	–	56,880
Portugal	7,222	13,751	12,318	33,291
Romania	335,706	120,000	80,000	535,706
Russia	1,700,000	5,000,000	–	6,700,000
Serbia	45,000	133,148	152,958	331,106
Turkey	250,000	400,000	–	650,000
USA	58,480	189,955	14,290	262,725
Totals	*7,996,888*	*21,755,196*	*1,979,556*	*31,508,200*

Index